Board Racing

Board Racing

Geoff Turner - Tim Davison

Photographs by Tim Hore

Fernhurst Books

First published 1982 by
Fernhurst Books, 13 Fernhurst Road, London SW6 7JN

ISBN 0 906754 06 2

Acknowledgements

The publishers gratefully acknowledge the help of
Performance Sailcraft (UK) Ltd in the preparation of
this book.
    Thanks are also due to Nick Hoare for his assistance
with the photo sessions in Weymouth Bay.
    The cover photograph is by Cliff Webb/Accolade
Photography and the cover design is by Margaret
Hallam.

Composition by Allset, London
Printed by Hartnoll Print, Bodmin

Contents

1 Equipment and tuning   7

The sail 8; the mast/sail combination 13;
the wishbone 14; harness lines 14; the
centreboard and skeg 15; the board 16;
clothing 17

2 Sailing technique   19

Beating 20; tacking 22; bearing away 28;
reaching 28; gybing 31; running 34

3 Race tactics and rules   37

The start 38; the beat 43; covering: attack
and defence 48; the windward mark 53;
the reach 54; the gybe mark 58; the
run 58; the leeward mark 61; the finish 62;
tides and currents 63

1 Equipment and tuning

THE SAIL

As the sail produces all the driving force for the board, it is crucial to get as much forward power out of it as possible. It helps to have a well cut sail to start with. In the one-design classes there's no choice of sails, but where you do have a choice, the best guide is the results list so if you are choosing a new sail, bear in mind what make the stars use. However, whatever sail you use, you must know how to set it up to best advantage.

The main checks you can make on the shape of the sail are:

1 The aerofoil section of the sail — how full the sail is, where the maximum fullness is and how fine the entry is (the amount of fullness in the front third of the sail). You can judge what type of section your sail has by drawing a camber line about two-thirds of the way up and at right angles to the luff sleeve. Use a marker pen and a straight edge.

2 The amount of twist in the sail — look from behind the sail when it's sheeted in to see how straight the leech is. If there's a lot of twist in the sail, the top third of the leech will fall away; if the leech is too tight, it will hook the top part of the sail to windward.

Sail controls

The sail shape can be altered dramatically by the way it is set up. The parameters controlling this are:

1 The outhaul tension
2 the downhaul (or cunningham) tension
3 the height of the wishbone on the mast.

The outhaul is used to control the fullness of the sail: the tighter the outhaul, the flatter the sail. The downhaul controls the position of maximum fullness: tightening the downhaul moves the flow further forward in the sail. Both these controls cause creases in the direction of their pull and remove creases at right angles to it — so to remove creases from the mast to the clew, either slacken the outhaul or tension the downhaul, and to remove creases down the luff of the sail, tighten the outhaul or loosen the downhaul. Any other creases are more difficult to deal with!

The effect of the height of the wishbone is more subtle: what it actually does is to alter the angle at which the outhaul is pulling. Raising the front of the wishbone makes the outhaul pull downwards more, which in turn tightens the leech of the sail, reducing the amount of twist. However, most sails do not allow much adjustment of the wishbone height and anyway it's uncomfortable to sail with a

A camber line (drawn on your sail with a marker pen and straight edge) will show the aerofoil section of your sail.

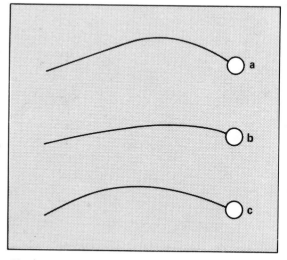

The aerofoil section of your sail may be full (a), flat (b) or full with a fine entry (c).

Parts of the sail.

A kicking strap (boom vang) also controls leech tension.

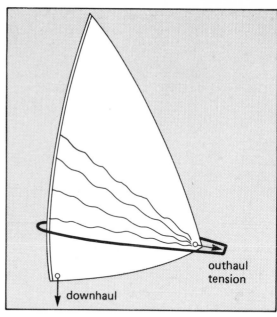

To cure creases, pull at right angles to them. In this case tighten the downhaul to remove the creases.

wishbone that's too high or too low: shoulder height is about right, but you should be able to move it up or down by about 10 cm.

The other way of controlling the leech tension is to use a kicking strap or boom vang — a line from the foot of the mast to the end of the wishbone. This can be very effective but it does have disadvantages: it tends to catch on the top of the centreboard when you tack and also, as the mast bends, the kicker slackens off and loses its effect — so it isn't too much use with a bendy mast or in gusty winds. Overall the use of a kicker isn't recommended.

The outhaul and downhaul should both be adjustable — don't use knots, use clam cleats and to make sure they won't slip, replace them when they start wearing out. It's adequate to have a 2:1 ratio on the downhaul, but 4:1 is better for the outhaul. If your wishbone has just the usual two pulleys in the end fitting, consider using them to give a 4:1 ratio with the outhaul line just going to one side of the wishbone — it's better to have an outhaul you can adjust easily from one side than one you can't adjust from either. Always put a figure-of-eight knot in the ends of the outhaul just in case it does manage to slip through the cleats.

You shouldn't need to alter the controls during a race unless the wind strength changes dramatically; the usual procedure is to set the sail up onshore and then to check it and make final adjustments while

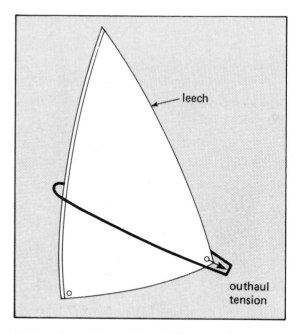

Raising the position of the wishbone on the mast tightens the leech.

sailing around before the race. When checking the settings onshore, remember that the rig is stationary so when the board is actually moving, the apparent windspeed will be 25 to 40 per cent higher. If you do adjust the settings before the start, leave enough time to check them with a quick beat before the start, and try to avoid making any changes after the 10-minute gun.

Setting up the sail

Now we know how the controls can alter the sail shape, what sail shape do we actually want?

The aim is to keep the airflow over the sail as smooth as possible. Usually you can't get smooth flow over both the windward and leeward sides of the sail at the same time, but in fact the leeward side is more important as that's the side that produces the lift. Any creases in the sail tend to prevent smooth flow. A certain amount of twist is necessary for two reasons: firstly, the wind is stronger 3 metres above the water than 1 metre above it, so the apparent wind is from further aft; secondly, the sail is narrower at the top so it can't deflect the air by so great an angle.

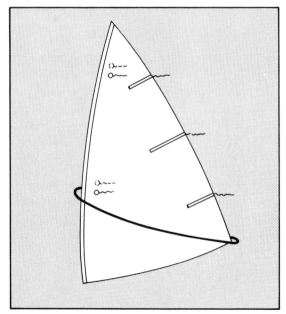

Position telltales on your sail as shown to indicate the wind flow.

Use telltales on the beat and close reach to see what the airflow's doing: if the airflow's smooth, they will fly with it; if not, they will just flutter or hang down. Have two pairs about 30 cm from the luff sleeve, one on each side just above the wishbone and the other pair about 1 metre from the head. Another three on the leech by the batten pockets can be useful also. However, when you're racing, don't become mesmerised watching the telltales. After a while you should be able to relate the feel of the rig to the way the telltales are behaving.

- If the sail is too full, the flow will break away on the leeward side of the sail making the sail stall. Telltales near the luff will be OK, but telltales on the batten pockets will be sucked round to the leeward side of the sail.
- If the sail is too flat, the telltales will look fine but the sail won't develop much lift and so will lack power.
- If the maximum fullness is too far forward, the front part of the sail will start backing (flapping) and the windward side telltales won't fly. It will be difficult to point high as the luff of the sail won't be doing much work.
- If the maximum fullness is too far back, the batten pocket telltales will again be sucked round to leeward. You'll find you need to hold the wishbone a long way back and the sail will feel very powerful — but unfortunately the power will be directed sideways rather than forwards.
- If there's the wrong amount of twist, it will be impossible to get both the lower and upper sets of telltales behaving the same way. Too much twist will let the top third of the sail fall away so it backs and doesn't produce any power when the rest of the sail is sheeted correctly; not enough will make it hook round and act as a brake. When there's the right amount of twist, the luff of the sail should start backing all the way up as you sheet the sail out.

Setting up the sail for particular conditions

In *medium winds*, set the sail up reasonably full but with enough outhaul tension to keep it clear of the wishbone. Tighten the downhaul as much as is necessary to get rid of the horizontal creases in the

Check the amount of twist in your sail ashore. Left: this sail has no twist. Centre: this sail has a large amount of twist — far more than the 10° which is the optimum for speed.

Right: the top of this sail is trimmed correctly; but because of excessive twist, the bottom has had to be trimmed too far to windward.

luff. There should be some twist in the sail but not a lot — when you look at the sail from behind, the leech should curve out about 20 cm from the vertical about a third of the way from the top. If there are waves, you'll need more power to deal with them, so set the sail a little fuller. You'll lose the ability to point so high, but it's worth it.

In *lighter winds*, keep the sail full but move the maximum fullness aft by slackening the downhaul until small horizontal creases appear in the luff. But in really light winds, too much fullness will make the sail stall so you need to start flattening it again by increasing the outhaul tension. This will probably make some nasty creases appear parallel to the wishbone, so increase the downhaul tension as well — but try to keep the fullness well aft all the same. There should now be very little twist in the sail — the leech should be almost vertical all the way up, but not to the extent of hooking over to windward.

In *stronger winds*, you need to flatten the sail and move the maximum fullness further forward, so put quite a lot of tension on both the outhaul and the downhaul. Set the wishbone as high up the mast as you can reach when sailing to reduce twist as much as possible, because the bend in the mast will let the sail twist enough anyway. In a real blow pull everything as tight as you can — try to get the sail as flat as a board. Once you're sailing, both the mast and wishbone will bend (probably permanently!) to put some shape back in the sail.

Change down to a smaller sail if you can't handle a full-size sail. Small sails can be faster for a number of reasons: they're easier to use as they're a flatter cut, and the clew is usually higher so the end of the wishbone doesn't hit the water so easily. Mainly, though, you won't fall off so often, so your performance is bound to improve. Usually a marginal is small enough (no battens, straight or hollow leech, straight foot) and the races in which a smaller storm sail is necessary are few and far between. Most events will allow the use of two sails, so it's a safe bet to choose a full-size sail and a marginal.

If the board has a choice of mast positions, have the mast forward in light winds so you can stand well forward to maximise waterline length. As the wind gets stronger, move the mast to the back position: once the board's planing, you will be standing further back so take the rig with you.

THE MAST/SAIL COMBINATION

Both masts and sailcloths can be soft (bendy, stretchy) or stiff, so try to get a sail that matches the mast, or vice versa. If the mast is too flexible for the sail, the sail will lose power in the gusts as the top half falls away to leeward; if the mast is stiff but the sailcloth too soft, the sail will not be able to handle the power and will set like a bag — very full with the maximum fullness a long way back — and the rig will be slow and difficult to use. Most sailcloth is fairly soft; a harder sail is either made from a stabilised cloth (e.g. CYT) or a laminate (e.g. Mylar). With masts, the general rule is that glass-fibre is softer (bendier) than alloy, although there are some epoxy masts that are as stiff as alloy but not as light. However, glass masts can take a lot more punishment than alloy as they don't stay bent and are relatively difficult to break outright; if you overstrain an alloy mast, the mast will either break or end up with a permanent bend. So if you're launching in surf using an alloy mast, make sure you've brought a spare!

Masts bend in different ways: most will curve evenly along their length but the better ones are stiffer at half height with the flex more in the top third. A sail will match the mast if the curve cut

Use a marginal sail if you find yourself falling off too often.

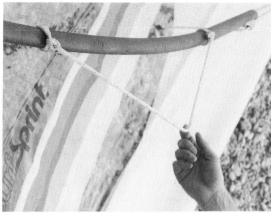

Tying a harness line to the wishbone.

A correctly positioned harness line.

into the luff of the sail matches the way the mast bends.

A soft rig is OK in light to medium winds and flat water, but a stiff rig is far better in wind and waves; in waves a lot of power is wasted on a soft rig flexing and unflexing the mast, while a stiff rig is always more predictable and so easier to use. The disadvantage of stiff rigs is that they tend to be heavier and therefore harder to pull from the water; however as development of masts and sailcloths continues, the rigs get lighter all the time.

A heavy sailor does put more strain on the rig so will need a stronger, stiffer rig than a lightweight.

THE WISHBONE

Whatever weight you are, the wishbone should always be stiff: there's no conceivable advantage in having a bendy one. Check a wishbone's stiffness by trying to pull the two sides apart; a good wishbone will have very little play — not more than 10 cm. If there is play, it often is caused by flexing in the end fittings rather than the wishbone itself so check these out — even if they're OK when the wishbone is new they can loosen after a month or two. The end fittings can usually be replaced on their own.

The wishbone should be tied to the mast as tightly as possible to give the rig a good stiff feel. The line attaching it takes a lot of strain so should be pretty strong and (like all other lines) replaced at the first signs of wear.

An oval section wishbone is generally considered easier on the hands and arms than a round one, but what's more important is the covering. A soft rough rubber is the best and anything smooth is to be avoided or roughened up. If you have to grip the wishbone hard to prevent it slipping through your hands, your arms will tire out in no time.

HARNESS LINES

Harness lines are there to take the strain of the sail, and should be positioned so that the middle of the harness line is by the centre of effort of the sail.

Three types of centreboard: retractable centreboard (left), pivoting daggerboard (centre) and daggerboard (right). Although the retractable version is complex, needing slot flushers, it is very pleasant to use. The daggerboard is simple, but must be pulled out downwind in a strong breeze.

This will be around 80 cm from the mast in medium winds, but it moves back as the wind increases. To get the right distance between the ends of the harness line, you need to have enough line to let the harness hook move around a bit, but if you have too much, the lines will tend to loop round the wishbone and waste valuable time when you try to hook in. If the ends are too close together, the harness can put a lot of strain on a short length of the wishbone, increasing the chance of bending it. The most usual distance between the ends of the line on the wishbone is 60 to 100 cm. The lines should be long enough to let you sail with your arms slightly bent so the hook should be about 40 cm from the wishbone. When you're buying harness lines, allow 150 cm for each line including the knots round the wishbone, or 100 cm if you have straps on the wishbone. The lines themselves should be stiff, hardwearing and certainly prestretched. Don't wait until they break before replacing them — it's very difficult to use a harness line with a knot in the middle.

THE CENTREBOARD AND SKEG

The centreboard should be well finished and with a good aerofoil section for minimum drag and optimum windward performance. If the shape of the centreboard is free, have one that's as deep as possible and with little or no rake — what is known as a 'high aspect' centreboard, i.e. long and thin. The centreboard should be a firm fit in the centreboard case with not more than 5 cm play in the tip and no twist. A loose centreboard will certainly not help windward performance, especially in waves; on the reach it will increase the tendency of the board to zap off in its own direction, and on the run a firm centreboard will make the board a lot less wobbly. Tighten up the fit of the centreboard by wrapping it with wide tape (e.g. carpet tape) or in really bad cases by gluing pieces of carpet tile on the centreboard or the inside of the case. However, if it's a pivoting daggerboard or centreboard, don't make it so tight that you end up breaking your toes kicking it back.

Unless you're using a fully retractable centreboard, make sure there's a strap on the top of the daggerboard so you can pull it out completely and hang it on your arm. The strap shouldn't cut into you and should be short enough to prevent the daggerboard spinning and applying a painful tourniquet to your elbow.

15

Try not to run the centreboard aground, and repair it if you do. Don't leave it lying flat in the sun — it can get warped remarkably quickly.

The shape of the skeg (fin) doesn't seem to be too important but its size does affect the board's manoeuvrability. A small skeg helps the board tack and gybe fast, while a large one gives the board more directional stability, which is useful when reaching fast in waves. So go for a compromise: a small skeg in shifty winds on flat water, but a larger one when conditions start getting hairy.

Like the centreboard, the skeg should be fairly stiff in its case or at speed it may start vibrating. Some plastic flip-up skegs are terrible, so chuck them away and replace them with something better if class rules allow it.

THE BOARD

Whatever type of board you sail, there are a few points that are always important:

1 The weight of the board. Don't let your board get heavier as it gets older, so always repair any damage that's going to let water in, and keep the board in a dry place when you're not using it.

2 The non-slip on the board should be effective. It's difficult to concentrate on a race if you're worried that your feet are going to disappear from under you. If the non-slip is doubtful, either roughen up the surface with a file (polyethylene boards only), paint the deck with special non-slip paint or rub on some wax. Wax is a good last-minute method, but make sure you use the right wax for the temperature as a soft wax will melt in the sun. Bear in mind that a non-slip that's fine for shoes may be useless in bare feet and vice versa, so don't switch between bare feet and shoes unless you're sure the non-slip is OK.

3 Keep the underside of the board in reasonable condition. It doesn't need to be perfect but it'll certainly seem faster if you've just spent a couple of hours smoothing out the scratches (use 600 grade wet-and-dry paper) or gluing on a new centreboard slot flusher.

4 The mast leash must be reliable and should never pull out or break when you're sailing.

CLOTHING

Harness. A bad harness can be pretty uncomfortable; all it will do is transfer the pain from your arms to your back, and back pain has a longer-lasting effect than aching arms ever do. So try to find one that puts the pull low down, in the small of the back rather than the shoulders, and that fits closely without crushing your ribs. Girls will find one designed especially for their sex more comfortable. Wear the harness tight enough so the hook doesn't lift more than 5 cm from your chest;

Three types of board: round (left), semi-displacement (centre) and flat (right). A round board is usually faster than a flat board especially in light winds and when beating because it points higher. However, these characteristics are achieved by sacrificing stability, strength and ease of handling — particularly in strong winds.

whether you have the hook pointing up or down is a matter of personal preference. To have it up stops the harness coming unhooked when you don't want it to but makes it harder to hook in the first place — so it really doesn't make much difference as long as you do the same each time. Always insist on a quick-release buckle so you can get out of the harness in an emergency, and if the harness doesn't have enough buoyancy for the rules, make sure you can wear it with a buoyancy aid as well.

Wetsuit. The purpose of the wetsuit is to keep you warm, which it can't possibly do unless it's a good fit. Suits made for windsurfing are usually of 3-4 mm neoprene; a smooth outer surface is warmer but more easily torn. The most popular combination is a sleeveless long-john, with a jacket for colder weather. Wearing anything tight on your arms makes them tire quicker. If it's really cold, a dry suit can work wonders but use it with discretion — they can be stiflingly hot on a reservoir in summer.

Shoes. Sailing barefoot can give you a good feel for the board, but shoes or boots give you better grip and keep your feet warm. The soles must be soft and flexible, and your feet should not be able to slide forward in the shoes, so they should be laced or at least tight across the bridge of your foot. Ankle support and protection is useful but not vital, so the choice between boots and shoes is up to you. Be wary of velcro fastenings: they're fine in the shop but can come loose when you're sailing.

2 Sailing technique

BEATING

In most races, about two-thirds of the time is spent beating so it's important to get the board going upwind as fast as possible. To succeed in doing this, you must know how close to the wind the board should be pointing – to point too high will cause the board to lose speed and drift sideways as the centreboard starts stalling, whereas sailing on a close reach, although very fast, will take a long time to get to the windward mark.

How close to sail depends partly on the board and partly on the wind and wave conditions. In general, a round displacement board with a high aspect (long and thin) centreboard will point higher than a flat board with a less efficient daggerboard, because the round board has greater lateral resistance, and won't slip sideways across the water so easily.

Beating in medium winds

The time to point highest is in a medium wind on flat water. Make sure the centreboard is fully down, and stand with your feet close together, either near the top of the centreboard or a little behind it. The back of the board should be just clear of the water and certainly not digging in. As a general rule, keep your hands as close together as possible on the wishbone (usually about 30 cm apart) and try to lean towards the front of the board, twisting your body so you're facing forwards and taking some of your weight on the wishbone. Always try to keep your legs and body straight, never leaning in towards the sail.

Flat boards are best sailed level so your back foot will be on the centreline and your front foot on the windward half of the deck. But on boards with a more rounded shape, it pays to rail (heel) them until the leeward edge is just touching the water — about 20 degrees. This has the effect of increasing the waterline length, reducing the wetted surface area

Beating in medium winds: pull the wishbone well in, stand with your feet together, hands 30 cm apart, leaning forwards. Try railing the board to improve pointing ability.

and increasing the angle of attack of the centre-board, so you go faster and point higher. To do this, try to hang from the rig to take your weight off the board, and press down with the toes of your back foot. The force on the daggerboard should then start the board railing; control the amount of railing by altering the pressure on your front foot.

The mast should either be vertical or leaning slightly towards the wind, so usually the wishbone would be at straight arm's length, but in the lighter moments you can bend your arms to get the rig nearer your body. Use a harness if you need to; it also helps transfer your weight from the board to the rig. Sheet the sail in so the end of the wishbone is over the leeward edge of the stern when the mast is vertical; as the mast starts leaning into the wind the end of the wishbone will move more over the centre or even the windward edge of the stern. Sheet the sail in so the luff is not quite backwinding, but fairly close to it — if you sheet the end of the wishbone out about half a metre the luff of the sail should start lifting. Usually the leeward side tell-tales will be flying but the windward ones just fluttering.

Try to keep body and sail movements to a mini-mum — you should only be trimming the sail in

In medium winds move your body in and out by bending and straightening your arms. The objective is to keep the mast steady and vertical. Only rake the mast to windward when you need to get your weight even further out.

response to small changes in the wind rather than as part of regular pumping. Take care not to oversheet the sail or it will stall and the board will stop dead — to get going again bear off for a few seconds before heading back up to closehauled.

Beating in medium winds and waves

Once waves start developing you need to change your technique, as you need more power and speed to make your way over them. If the board is sailing too close to the wind, the waves will slow it down and occasionally stop it dead. So bear off to try to keep the board moving fast. To help this, set the sail up so it's fuller and more powerful than it would be for flat water. Don't try to force the board through the waves but let it ride over them. In order to do this, the board must be free to move under your feet, so let the rig take as much of your weight as it can, and keep your feet close together so that the weight that's left on them won't prevent the bow and stern from lifting with the waves. However, in a short chop the board may start ploughing through the waves rather than over them so there's always water washing over the deck. Try to prevent this by standing further aft, lifting the bow high enough to stay above most of the waves. Again, a round board will cut through the waves better when it's sailed slightly on its rail.

As the waves get steeper it's best to start taking more notice of them, so as you climb up the wave, luff up to get over the hill and then bear off as you go down the other side. If there's a particularly nasty wave coming, try to sail round it rather than through it.

Beating in light winds

In light winds, concentration becomes very important as the wind will tend to shift, and once the board has stopped, it takes ages to get the speed back again. So always try to keep the sail trimmed as well as possible and watch for the first signs of the sail starting to lift as you go too close to the wind, or feel the power going from the sail as you oversheet it. If the board is pointing too high, it'll lose what little speed it has and the centreboard will start stalling. It isn't easy to feel that; the most obvious sign is that the board starts drifting sideways, and the only way to cure it is to bear away until the board gains some speed, and then luff up again — but not so near the wind this time. The rig should be as close to vertical as possible; this often means adopting the 'kangaroo' position with the wishbone right up against your chest, which can become very uncomfortable after a while as your elbows start to seize up. You'll need to stand further forward on the board in order to get the maximum length of the board in the water, with the minimum wetted area. Usually this will mean letting the stern just touch the water, and even on flat boards it may pay to start railing them.

It's essential to keep the board steady, so move around as little as possible. If you do need to do something like looking over your shoulder, do it smoothly and don't let it break your concentration. If there are any sort of waves at all, you'll

In light winds stand well forward, rail the board and keep the rig vertical by using the kangaroo grip.

need all the power you've got to get the board over them so add to it by giving a slight pump as the board climbs the wave.

Beating in strong winds

In strong winds, differences in speed upwind can be very noticeable and a beat that takes the leaders 15 minutes may take the less experienced twice as long. The most obvious reason for this is that the leaders don't fall in while the others take dips to

Don't be afraid to use a small sail if you have trouble with a full-sized one — a small one sheeted in properly is better than a large one only half working. However, as you get better and stronger, you'll find yourself using a small sail less and less.

TACKING

The races where it's best to sail the windward leg in one tack are few and far between; usually many tacks are necessary, so it's worth while learning to tack consistently well.

First, having decided you want to tack, choose the exact moment. Try to time it so the board doesn't hit any waves head on; so look for a smaller wave than usual, start luffing as you climb it and perform the tack as you're going down the back.

Start by unhooking yourself from the harness, then sail the board up into the wind by raking the sail back and sheeting in until it's just past the centreline. Don't sheet in too fast or too far or the board will stop dead — it'll make for a quick tack but at the expense of a length or two of distance upwind. In windier conditions, push with your back foot to dip the leeward rail and help the board turn. Once the board has turned just past head to wind, jump round the mast putting your front foot on the other side. With your back hand, grab the mast or the front of the wishbone — not the uphaul line. By now the board should have turned almost to the new closehauled direction so move aft while throwing the rig forwards into the wind. Catch the wishbone with both hands, hook into the harness and sheet in as the board accelerates. If you sheet in too fast the sail will stall, eventually making the board start drifting slowly sideways. If you can't hook in first time, leave it to sort out later — when you're coming out of the tack it's more important to get the board moving again. If something goes wrong and the board is almost stationary, bear away further than usual and give the sail a couple of hard pumps before hardening up again.

In stronger winds use your feet more when turning the board — push on your back foot to turn the board into the tack and, once you're on the other side, use your front foot to bear away. Make

sure you move far enough back as you sheet in to prevent the front of the board going under the water.

Of course some boards tack faster than others. Although it's always possible to tack a board fast, it's usually best not to try and force it round faster than it wants to go. However if you do need to do a crash tack — that board on starboard suddenly seems to be rather close! — you will need to force the board round by jumping back and sheeting in fast but after the tack bear well away to get going again and to prevent the other board sailing past you to windward.

Practise tacking until every one is almost perfect. Even if you mess up just one tack in five, you can be sure that will be the tack that really matters.

windward — mistakes that become more frequent as they get tired (partly from pulling the rig out of the water each time).

However there is more to it than just staying upright. To get maximum speed out of the board it must be kept planing, so bear off a little and move your weight well back — stand with your front foot level with the back of the daggerboard case. Similarly, move your hands and, if necessary, the harness lines further down the wishbone. Your back hand will be close to the jam cleat and your front hand about 40 cm from the mast so the pull on each arm is about the same. If you find your front arm tires quickly, try using an underhand grip on the boom. Rake the mast well back and sheet in really hard so the foot of the sail is almost horizontal and parallel to the centreline. To prevent the board luffing up, put more pressure on your front foot by leaning well forward.

Railing can be a problem because when the board is moving really fast, the lift generated by the centreboard becomes more than the board can resist and the board capsizes to leeward. To prevent this happening, the first thing to do is to maximise the force keeping the board level, by moving both your feet out until you're standing on the windward edge of the board, and pressing down as much as possible. But if it still rails, more drastic measures are necessary — you've got to reduce the lift from the centre-

board. If you can point higher and still keep planing, do it. By slowing the board down it may stay the right way up. If not, the only remedy is to reduce the area and/or depth of the centreboard by raising it, usually just a few centimetres but in really strong winds maybe halfway up. If it's a pivoting one, this has the added bonus of moving the area back as well.

Falling in to windward is usually caused by sheeting out the rig — probably as a gust hits and your back hand just can't hold the wishbone in hard enough. As the sail is sheeted out, the pull of the sail moves forward and it loses lift. But you've still got all your weight pulling the rig over to windward, so that's the way it goes. The way to avoid this is therefore either not to sheet out: really hold that rig in hard, using the harness to take a lot of the strain; or alternatively, as you do sheet out, make sure that you get your weight more over the board. Often you can see gusts coming from the ripples on the water; you can prepare for a gust by pulling the rig nearer your body so when it comes you still have some reserve in your arms: you can let them straighten as the gust hits. The board should be planing the whole time; if it's not you're probably pointing too high so bear off enough to get it going and move your weight well back.

If you do go in to windward, getting going again can take a while. As you climb back on the board and wearily start pulling the rig out again, keep calm and don't rush it. Be ready for the sail to swing violently round to leeward and, when it does go, try hard to keep the end of the boom out of the water or else it will be blown straight back down on the leeward side. Get the board pointing on a close-hauled course again, put your hands back on the wishbone and then in one smooth movement pull the rig forward and to windward, move aft on the board and sheet in. If you immediately go straight back in to windward, you didn't sheet in hard enough (try again!); if you go in to leeward, you hadn't got the rig far enough to windward before sheeting in.

Try to stop the board railing too much by standing on the windward rail, slowing a little or raising the centreboard. Right: beating in strong winds.

BEARING AWAY

At the windward mark, it often seems that the board just won't bear away onto the reach or the run. What happens is that the board will bear off to a beam reach, then accelerate hard and start to luff up again, or it will bear off well to a broad reach and just when everything seems fine the rig will pull you over the bow.

There are two factors which influence turning the board: the position of the rig, and the attitude of the board. To make it bear away, the rig must be raked well forward and the board needs to be tilting to windward. So when you're ready to bear away, pull the rig well over you by bending your arms. Then move it further forward and start to heel the board by pushing down the windward edge. The board should start turning away from the wind. As it does, sheet the sail out but still keep the rig well over to windward. Try not to move your weight too far forward or the bow might start burying itself in the waves. Once the board is on a reach it will start moving fast — this is when there's a danger of luffing up again. To prevent that, just stay as you are with the rig over to windward and the board heeling. Avoid the temptation to sheet the sail back in. Once the board is through the beam reach position, you're relatively safe. It will slow down a little which will make the sail pull harder, so move your weight further back and turn from

facing across the board to facing forward. You can then breathe a sigh of relief and start looking for the next mark.

In stronger winds you may need to kick the centreboard back or even pull it right out for the offwind leg. If you can just kick it back, leave it until after you've borne away as the board will turn tighter with the centreboard down. However, if you need to pull it out completely, it's easier to do it before you bear away. Let go of the boom with your back hand and hold it well forward to start the board turning. Lean down and grab the daggerboard strap with your back hand, pull it out and get your hand back on the boom, flicking the daggerboard strap onto your arm. Then sheet in and continue bearing away.

REACHING

Reaching is the point of sailing that causes the least trouble; after all, when you're not racing, what else do you do except reach back and forth? However, a good distance can be gained on the reach if you can make your board move just that much faster than the others. Reaching technique is fairly straight-forward: move your weight back as far as you can without causing the stern to start dragging; if you have a pivoting centreboard, raise it to around half

28

Right: reaching.

up (it's usually best to leave non-pivoting dagger-boards fully down); and keep the board level. The technique that makes the crucial difference to the board's speed is the ability to catch the waves — not just the occasional one but every single one there is.

As a wave starts lifting the board from behind, bear away so the board is pointing straight down it. The rules allow you three pumps to get your board surfing, so use them. Once you're on a wave, do your best to stay with it, which may mean going up to 30 degrees off your usual course. If you're moving faster than the wave, luff up in order to reach along it; if you're slower keep going straight down it. When you do eventually lose the wave, the board will be sailing uphill so luff up a little to get the bow off the back of the wave and into the trough. Then look for the next wave; when it starts to lift you, start the process again.

In light winds, the only difference is that there's no need to retract the centreboard and of course it helps to keep movements to a minimum.

Reaching in strong winds

When reaching in strong winds, the biggest problem is to keep the board travelling in the right direction, as once it's started going off course it's difficult to regain control — and just a few seconds in the water can mean losing a large distance. So, to keep it going in the direction you want, don't have any more

centreboard down than is necessary. Usually, the
centreboard can be almost fully up on a broad
reach, and no more than half down on a close reach.
Even when kicked right back a pivoting daggerboard may still cause problems so when travelling
very fast you may want to pull it out. Get your
weight well back and stand with your feet separated
— on a close reach your front foot on the windward
edge of the board, your back foot in the middle; on
a broad reach, one foot on each side. Then try to
control the direction of the board by steering with
your feet, heeling the board to windward to bear
away and to leeward to luff up. It's quite OK to use

On a reach, move your weight back (without
dragging the stern). Raise the centreboard
halfway and steer with your feet: press on the
windward rail to turn away from the wind
and vice versa.

a harness on a close reach, but more dangerous, and not so necessary, on a broad reach.

Keep an eye open for the gusts. When you see a gust coming get ready for it by bending your arms to get the rig close to you; as the gust hits bear away and sheet out, sheeting in again as the board accelerates. If you find yourself being pulled over the front, sheet out more, but don't overdo it or the rig will fly in to windward taking you with it. As the gust passes, harden up again to get yourself back on the course to the mark.

If you fall off to windward try not to let go of the rig until the board has stopped — it can be disastrous if the board disappears into the distance leaving you swimming. If you fall in to leeward you'll probably land on top of the sail which stops the board pretty quickly, as long as the mast leash doesn't pull out. If you don't have a mast leash, you've got serious problems as the board is quite likely to drift faster than you can swim and your only real hope is that someone will pick you up before you're exhausted. However if you do fall off, it's easiest to get going again from the beam reach position and then bear off if you need to. Pull the rig well forward and to windward with your front hand before grabbing the boom with your back hand, moving your front hand onto the boom, leaning back and sheeting in. The board will accelerate fast so sheet in as it does and you should be OK again — ready to regain those lost places.

GYBING

In most races, you'll probably only need to gybe a few times — at the wing mark, at the start or end of the run and possibly once or twice during the run. On the other hand, you can lose a lot of ground if you mess up just one of your gybes, far more than by tacking badly, so practise hard to get your gybes right. It can be very satisfying to complete a perfect high-speed gybe straight from one fast reach to another!

The standard gybe is from a broad reach to a broad reach. Let's follow a gybe from port to starboard (see photo sequence). To turn the board well, use your feet as much as the sail. Start bearing away

by pulling the rig well over to windward and sheeting the sail out until the luff is almost lifting. Press down on your left foot to dip the windward rail and as the board turns onto the run, jump back to stand facing forward with one foot on each side of the board — but still with most pressure on your left foot to keep the board heeling that way. Let the board sail right through the wind by keeping the rig tilted over to windward — the mast may be as much as 45 degrees from the vertical and, as you're now sailing clew first, the sail will be sheeted out past 90 degrees. Then gybe the sail by letting go with your right hand and pulling the rig to the right with your left hand. As the wishbone swings over the front of the board cross your right hand over or under your left and grab either the mast or the other side of the wishbone. Let go with your left hand and, once you have pulled the mast far enough to windward, catch the wishbone with the left hand. Now sheet in and sail on.

As you're gybing, change the position of your feet ready for the new side: move your front foot forward and your back foot into the centre of the board so you're facing across the board again, rather than forward. Level the board off again to stop it luffing up too far.

Don't let the sail stop when it's pointing downwind — the change from one tack to the other should be one smooth movement. It's important not to gybe the sail too early; if you gybe it when the board's pointing dead downwind, it's difficult to get the board to turn any further, so leave it until the board has already turned through the wind.

In light winds, railing the board has less effect in helping the board to turn, so use the sail more. As you gybe the sail, instead of just letting the sail swing round with the wind, actually push it round with your back hand. As you sheet in on the new tack, keep the rig tilted well back, so the clew of the sail is almost touching the water, and don't sheet in too fast or the sail will stall. Keep the board railing to leeward so it keeps turning, and give a couple of pumps as you sheet in to help the board get round.

In stronger winds, turn the board more with your feet than with the sail. You can turn the board amazingly fast by doing a 'flare gybe': as the board is turning from the broad reach to the run, jump right back on the board and press hard on your

Above: a standard gybe from port to starboard (see page 31). Bear away by pulling the rig to *windward and sheeting out the sail. Weight on the left foot dips the windward rail helping the*

The stop gybe (page 34). Push the sail out so it backs, and keep pushing till the board stops. *Then start pulling the sail round, using your feet to help swivel the board. Keep pressure on*

board turn. Let the board sail right through the turn before gybing the sail, then flatten the board to stop it luffing up too far and sheet in on the new side.

the sail to keep the board turning. Then give a couple of hard pumps to get going again.

windward foot so the back of the board sinks. The board will then start spinning; as it goes, move your feet so you're ready for the new tack, and then gybe the sail. It will flick round very fast, so catch it as it goes and sheet in straight away. Change the pressure from your back foot to your front foot to level the board off and stop it turning too far; once you're pointing in the right direction, lean back and go.

When gybing at the end of a run, you'll need to turn the board right round until it's beating. To keep the board luffing after you've gybed, don't level the board off as you gybe the sail, but keep it railed by pressing down on your leeward foot, and keep your weight well back so the stern is almost under the water. As the board luffs up past a reach, keep the rig tilted well back and pump the sail slightly to keep the board turning. Once the board has luffed up to the beat, move your weight forward and level the board off again.

In light winds it's not so easy to do a really tight turn. If it's particularly important that your gybe is tight — for example, when gybing in a small gap between another board and the wing mark — try doing a 'stop gybe', so called because the board will stop dead as you do it. The stop gybe relies entirely on using the sail to turn the board. Keep your weight around the mast step so the stern of the board is lifted clear of the water, and start the gybe by stopping the board — push the sail out so it backs, and keep pushing. Once the board has stopped, switch your hand to the other side of the wishbone and start pulling the sail round. Try to swivel the board with your feet; as the board turns shuffle your feet around the mast, and keep the pressure on the sail to keep the board turning. Once you're round, the board will be stationary, so give a couple of hard pumps to get it going again. Only do a stop gybe if you're in a tight corner, and don't expect it to be too successful on a board that doesn't turn fast anyway.

If you're gybing halfway down the run, you should use a slightly different technique as you don't need to turn the board much, just the sail. Start the gybe with a pump; tilt the rig over to windward and pull in with your front hand. Then let go with your back hand and move it onto the mast. Pull the rig across to the other side of the

board, move your free hand onto the other side of the wishbone and sheet in fast on the new gybe with another pump. In light winds, this manoeuvre should cause no problems and the two pumps you give can actually increase your speed; however it's a different story in strong winds and large waves as it can be difficult to get the sail sheeted in again on the new gybe. Try to keep the board moving fast throughout the gybe, so do it while you're surfing down a wave. The critical point is when you try to sheet in the sail; make it easier by pulling the rig well back as you change gybes, and sheet in fast. As you sheet in, the sail will pull hard so have your weight well back and be ready for it.

RUNNING

Running is the leg of the course that gives the most problems. In easy conditions — light to medium winds and no waves — there's no problem about sailing the board, but the only way to go faster than anyone else is by pumping, which is of course illegal. In stronger winds or waves, the problem changes and just staying on the board becomes difficult, especially on the less stable displacement boards.

In light to medium winds, stand fairly well forward, around the front of the centreboard case, to keep the back of the board from dragging in the water — it should be touching the water or just clear of it. Keep the board level with both your feet close to the centreline. The sail should be square on to the wind with the mast vertical or tilted slightly forward. Keep your arms bent so the wishbone stays close to your chest, and if you've got long harness lines, loop them round the wishbone so you don't inadvertently get hooked in. Leave the centreboard down; if you have it up, the board will be less stable and less responsive to alterations in the trim which make it change direction.

Running in strong winds

In strong winds the main cause of falling off on the run is lack of practice. The first step in learning to survive the run is getting the board to go in a straight line. In medium winds, when you'll be

Running in light winds. Stand well forward with your feet splayed, Chaplin style. Keep your arms bent.

35

*Running in strong winds. Pull the daggerboard
out or retract the centreboard.*

surfing down waves but not planing otherwise,
swivel the centreboard about half back — not too
much or the board will become too unstable. If the
daggerboard doesn't pivot, leave it right down. If
there's enough wind to keep the board planing the
whole time, you can retract the centreboard fully or
pull the daggerboard right out; the board will be
more stable when it's planing the whole time. Steer
the board with your feet: if you want to bear away,
tilt the board to windward; if you want to luff up,
tilt it to leeward. But generally, if you keep the
board level, it will go in a straight line so keep your
weight central. It's best to stand with your feet
splayed — your heels fairly close together but your
toes pointing out towards the edge of the board.
That way, you can correct the board if it starts to
rail by pressing down with your toes on the opposite side, but you're less likely to overcorrect and
start it railing the other way, getting into a see-saw
motion, first on one rail, then the other, then in
the water. Stand well back, behind the daggerboard
case, to give the board more stability and to stop
the bow from burying. In choppy seas, you will
need to move backwards and forwards to keep the

board trimmed correctly: as a wave picks you up,
move forward to get the board surfing down it;
once you're going fast, move back again, and as
the board comes off the wave and starts hitting the
one in front, move your weight well back to lift
the bow and prevent it from carving into the
water. Try to keep surfing as much as possible, so
steer the board to stay on the wave and to avoid
any particularly steep ones in front.

When the board is surfing, the sail will pull less
hard as the apparent wind decreases; it may even
start backing if you're going particularly fast, so just
hold it there and concentrate on steering the board
with your feet. But as the board comes off the
wave, the sail will get the wind back, so in order to
stop it pulling you over the front, bend your arms
to get the rig well back over your body. It's not a
good idea to use a harness on the run, so again loop
the harness lines over the wishbone to stop yourself
getting hooked in by mistake. When a gust hits and
the sail starts pulling too hard, don't sheet out as
that will make the sail go over to windward, taking
you with it. Don't sheet in either, or the sail will
probably pull you in to leeward, which isn't a whole
lot better. What you need to do is to move back on
the board, so the sail is pulled more over you, still
square on to the wind but giving more lift and less
pull.

If you do manage to stay on the board, the run
will be over quite quickly so you can look forward
to the final beat; however, if you do fall in, it's very
difficult to get sailing again on a dead run. Put the
daggerboard down before you try to pull the rig
out — it'll make it much easier to stand on the
board. Get the rig out of the water with the board
in a beam reach direction, then swivel it round to
point on a broad reach. Either kick the centreboard back, or pull the daggerboard out with your
back hand while holding the front of the wishbone
or the mast with your front hand. Then pull
the rig backwards and to windward; put your back
hand on the wishbone, then your front hand and
sheet in. Don't sheet in too fast or the rig will pull
you over, and as the board starts moving, bear off
onto a run by keeping the rig over to windward and
railing the board with your windward foot. Once
the board is on the run, move back again and stand
facing forwards.

3 Race tactics and rules

In this part of the book, each stage of the race is discussed in turn. For each stage the overall race strategy is given first, assuming that there are no other competitors around and that you can sail where you want. Then we go on to acknowledge the presence of other boards which will force you to modify your 'ideal' strategy and describe the board-to-board tactics you can use to beat them.

The course

The usual course used in serious regattas is the Olympic course, made up of a beat followed by a number of alternating 'triangles' and 'sausages'. The race usually begins near the leeward mark and ends near the windward mark, giving a high proportion of beating.

Normally, there will be a briefing session for competitors before you go on the water for the first race; it's a good idea to arrive in time for this! Make sure that before you go afloat you know the course, the type of start, and which way the marks should be rounded.

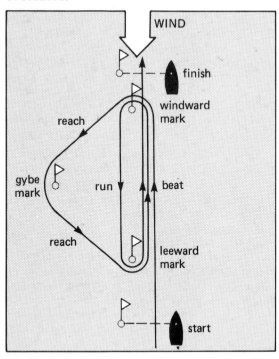

An Olympic type course, marks to port.

The rules

The rules for boardsailing races have been laid down by the International Yacht Racing Union (IYRU). It's well worth buying a copy from your national authority and studying it. Most common collisions (and near misses) are dealt with in the following pages, but there's really no substitute for studying the rule book.

THE START

The thirty seconds before and after the start are the most important minute of the race. A good start gets your sail forward of the fleet into clean wind; you can tack on windshifts (page 44) and only have to use defensive tactics to stop your opponents getting past. To do this you need to cross the line at the right place with full speed just after the gun, well clear of your nearest neighbours!

If you're serious about getting a good start, you will need a reliable, waterproof stopwatch.

The two types of start described here are the *line start* and the *gate start*.

The line start

Most races are started on a beat. The race committee sets a start line usually between the mast of the committee boat and a buoy. They often lay another buoy, which does not have to be on the line, near the committee boat, and boards are not allowed to sail between this buoy and the committee boat.

Ten minutes before the start the class flag (or a white shape) is raised on the committee boat and a gun is fired.

Five minutes before the start the blue peter (or a blue shape) is raised and a gun is fired.

At the start, both flags are lowered (or a red shape is raised) and a gun is fired. Boards must be behind the start line when the starting gun is fired.

Sometimes a gun is also fired one minute before the start. You then must keep behind the line for the final minute.

Getting a good start. Set your watch at the ten-minute gun, and check it at the five-minute gun.

Don't go too far from the line — 30 metres is plenty (p. 63 tells you what to do if there is a tide running). A wall of boards builds up on the line in the last two minutes, and you must be in that wall. If you're behind it, not only can you not get in, but your wind is cut off by the other sails.

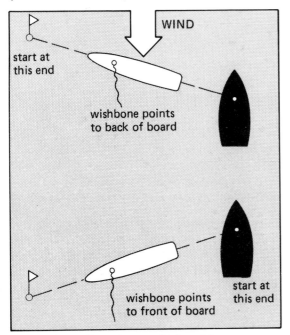

A biased start line: choose which end to start by pointing the board down the line and holding the rig by the uphaul line so it swings freely.

The start line is between the committee boat mast (A) and the buoy (B). Boards are not allowed to sail between buoy C (not on the line) and A.

Aim to be three or four lengths behind the line with 45 seconds to go — even closer if the line is crowded. You must be on starboard tack — on port tack you have no rights and are sure to be hit by another board and protested. Control your speed very carefully using the wishbone. Keep the board creeping forward as slowly as you can — most of the sail will be flapping. With ten seconds to go, you should be one length behind the line. Pull in the wishbone, lean back and start beating. You should then cross the line just after the gun with full speed.

Which end of the line should I start? If the wind is at right angles to the start line it doesn't matter where on the line you start — the middle is as good as anywhere (although if you plan to go up one side of the beat, perhaps because of the tide, then start near that end of the line).

Usually, however, the wind is *not* at right angles to the line and you must start at the end which is furthest to windward. To find out which end this is, point your board down the line, holding the rig by the uphaul rope so that the sail flaps freely: the far end of the wishbone will lie nearer the front or the back of the board. If the wishbone lies towards the *back* of the board, then the board is pointing towards the favoured end of the line; if the wishbone lies towards the *front* of the board, the board

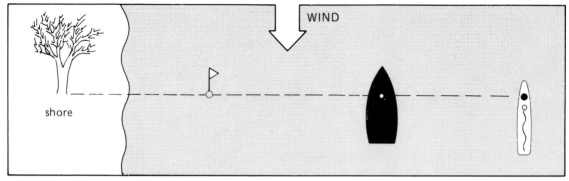

Taking a transit. When the buoy and the tree line up exactly you will know you are on the start line.

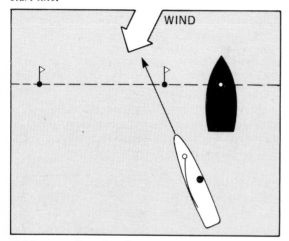

Making a starboard end start.

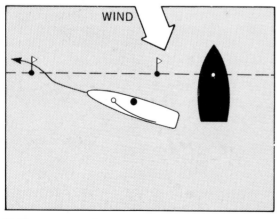

Making a port end start.

is pointing towards the wrong end of the line.

Repeat this manoeuvre a few times during the ten minutes leading up to the start. Once you're convinced which end of the line is best, go for a start near that end.

Making a starboard end start. Sail slowly, and as close to the wind as possible so you will reach the windward end of the line with the gun. Boards to windward of you have no rights (shout 'keep clear!' if they try to barge in) and will be forced out. Boards to leeward can't touch you — you are already sailing as close to the wind as possible.

Making a port end start. Keep near the port end of the line. Aim to cross as near the buoy as possible. Tack onto port tack as soon as you can clear the fleet. Never start on port tack unless the line is so biased that you can't even sail down it on starboard tack.

How do I know I'm on the line? Just after the ten-minute gun, look down the start line from behind the committee boat mast. Try to pick out a fixed object (e.g. a tree) which lies on an extension of the line. The tree and buoy form a *transit*. Later, when you are about to start, you can line up the buoy and tree (or whatever) and know when you're on the line. If there's no suitable object to the left of the line, you may be able to get a transit from the other end.

Watch carefully during the ten minutes leading up to the start — the committee may move the line, or the boat (or buoy) may drag its anchor; in which case take another transit.

40

Avoiding protests at the start

In the middle of the line the board to leeward of you has right of way. For example, in the figure below board G must keep clear of board I, who can turn slowly towards G. You have rights over the board to windward, and can turn towards it (G can edge up to H).

At the starboard end of the line boards to windwards are not allowed to barge in at the mark. Board D, for example, can't push between board E and mark C. Danger area X has become known as 'coffin corner' for this reason.

At the port end of the line you cannot tack if it looks as if you're going to hit the mark. Board I will be lucky to clear mark B — all it can do is sail as close to the wind as possible, and hope! Board F has no chance except to tack onto port and sail behind the fleet — area Y is the second danger area to avoid.

Sailing backwards is OK, but you have *no* rights over other boards.

Dropping the rig into the water between the preparatory signal (e.g. the five-minute gun) and the start is not allowed. You will have to satisfy the race committee that you dropped the rig in unintentionally and that you pulled it up as soon as possible.

While raising the rig from the water you have *no* rights until the sail is full of wind.

How can I 'kill' the other boards?

As you line up to start, keep turning into the wind a little. This keeps you away from the board to leeward — it also opens up a nice 'hole' to leeward that you can sail down into at the start (for extra speed). This hole is essential — there's nothing worse than starting with a rival just below you, because his lee-bow effect (p. 48) will stop you dead. Once you've made your hole (by turning into the wind) protect it jealously. If you see some one else heading for the gap, rotate your board so it points along the line with the sail flapping. This closes the gap and discourages the intruder (although you will have to keep clear of him once he is overlapping you to leeward).

Above all, don't reach down the line with 15 seconds to go like board J. You will have no rights over G, H and I who will sail into you. If you're too early, let the sail out and slow down.

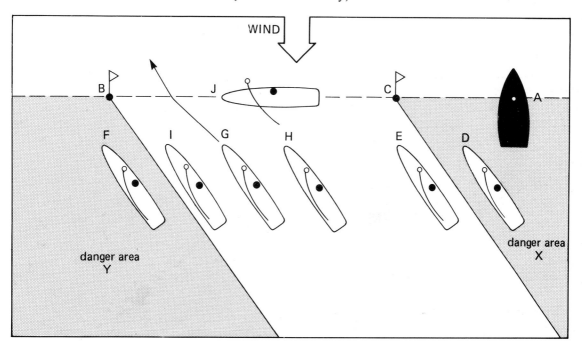

41

The gate start

A gate start is made by crossing the wake of a board called the pathfinder which is beating on port tack in front of the fleet. In theory everyone has an equally good start, because the earlier you start the further you have to sail.

The pathfinder, who is selected by the race committee from among the competitors, waits near the committee boat while the usual sound and flag signals are made. About one minute before the start the pathfinder sets off on port tack, accompanied by two motor boats, the gate boat and the guard boat, to protect it from over-enthusiastic competitors. A few seconds before the start a free-floating buoy is dropped over the back of the gate boat to mark the left-hand end of the line. After the start competitors (on starboard tack) pass closely behind the gate boat. The line gradually lengthens, and the boards start one at a time. A late start is no disadvantage, since the pathfinder is sailing up the beat for you while you're waiting.

Getting a good start. You need to know the course the pathfinder will take. So, with about four minutes to go, begin beating on port tack from the committee boat. After two or three minutes bear away onto a reach, then tack and wait with your sail flapping (like board G in the figure below). Watch for the pathfinder, and control your speed so that you beat slowly up to the stern of the guard boat. As you go behind it, pick up speed by bearing away slightly and then beat, flat out, to pass just behind the stern of the gate boat.

Never reach towards the guard boat like board F. You have no rights over boards D and E who will push you into the guard boat or gate boat. If you hit either, you will be disqualified. If you find yourself in board F's position, try to tack onto port and bear away. When you're ready, tack back onto starboard and try again. If all else fails, point into the wind and stop!

How can I recover from a bad start? If you start too far from the gate boat, your only option is to sail through the gate, then tack onto port and sail behind the whole fleet to the right-hand side of the course. If that turns out to be the best side, you could find yourself ahead at the windward mark!

When should I start? Start late if you're slower

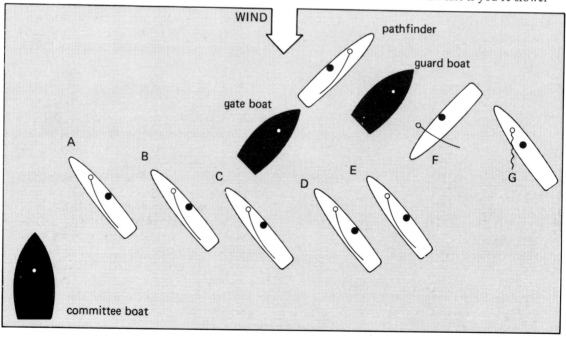

A line start — don't reach down the line with 15 seconds to go!

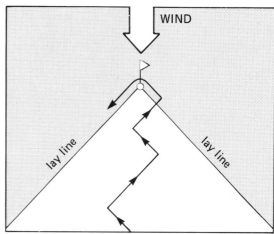

A lay line is the path you would sail along closehauled to hit the windward mark.

than the pathfinder, if you think the pathfinder will hit a permanent header (page 44) or if the tide is more favourable to the right-hand side of the course.

THE BEAT

After a good start you'll have to sail on starboard tack for a while, because the other boards will prevent your tacking. Try to inch ahead of your opponents to be ready to tack on the first windshift (see below). If no shift comes, consider tacking after a few minutes anyway, to stay ahead of the centre of the fleet.

The only way to recover from a *bad* start is to tack onto port and sail (close) behind the fleet. Tack back when a gap appears. If no gap materialises, you'll have to sail right behind the lot and bank on the starboard side of the course paying off. In fact, you don't lose much by this manoeuvre

since the wind is deflected in your favour by the starboard tack boards crossing you.

Lay lines

A *lay line* is the path you would sail along close-hauled to hit the windward mark. Avoid the lay lines like the plague: if you're outside them you have overstood the mark — you have sailed extra distance and will have to reach back to the mark.

The first beat

Unless you are *sure* that one side of the beat is favoured, make fairly short tacks (200 metres) up the middle. Shorten the tacks as you approach the windward mark. This method leaves you free to take advantage of windshifts.

Some sailors zoom off to one side on the first beat — they *might* be first at the windward mark, but they're more likely to be last. It's nice to be first, of course, but a position in the top quarter of the fleet is safer and, particularly in a series of races, you can't afford to risk a chancey first beat.

As you approach the windward mark, note who's ahead and try to work out why their route was fastest. If you're sure it was their *route* and not just their *speed*, consider going that way next time.

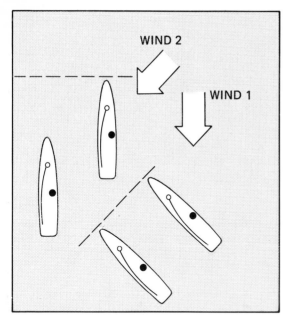

Spotting a windshift: you will pull ahead of a leeward board if the wind lifts.

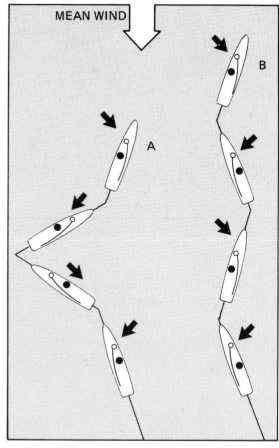

Board A takes no account of windshifts: note how little progress it makes compared with B.

After a couple of beats it will become clear which side of the course is fastest — the more confident you are, the further that way you can go on subsequent beats.

Windshifts

Once you have good speed and can tack efficiently, you are ready to start using windshifts.

The wind constantly alters in direction about its average. Some of the shifts are more pronounced and last longer than others — it is these that you have to spot and use.

You can tell if the wind has shifted by watching your course relative to a point on the shore (or a mark). If you're beating out at sea, you'll have to rely on how you're pointing relative to other boards. If the wind *lifts* (enables you to sail more directly to the windward mark), you pull ahead of boards to leeward and should continue to sail on the same tack. The opposite is true of *headers* (windshifts forcing you to alter course away from the mark) and you should tack.

In shifty winds, stay close to the middle of the beat and tack each time the wind heads you. The board A in the figure above takes no account of windshifts; note how little progress it makes compared with the board B, which tacks each time the wind heads it.

The main problem is to differentiate between a real shift and a short-lived change in the wind. For that reason, sail on into each shift for five or ten seconds to make sure it's going to last. If a header lasts that long, tack. If you find yourself tacking too often, or are confused, sail on one tack for a while until you're sure what the wind is doing. Remember that you lose a length each time you tack, so there has to be a good reason to do so.

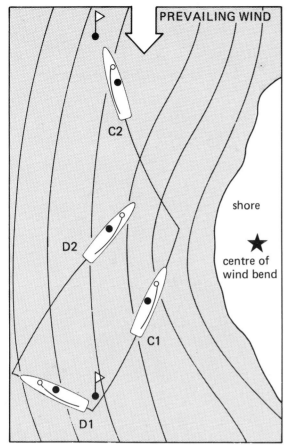

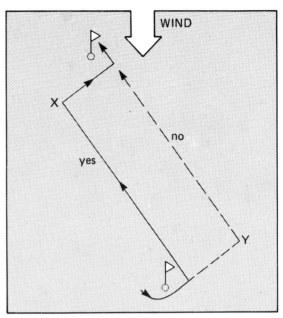

On a one-sided beat, sail the long leg first.

A wind bend, caused by the shore in this example, can lift you on both tacks if you sail towards its centre.

Don't sail right out to the lay lines — if you do and the wind shifts, you will lose ground because you can't take advantage of a lift, or tack on a header.

Wind bends

Unlike windshifts, which oscillate back and forth, a wind bend is (as its name implies) a steady change in wind direction from one end of the course to the other.

Wind bends can be caused by hills, or a change in the weather. Whatever the cause, sail towards the centre of the bend. In the figure above, the wind bend is caused by the shore. Board C, taking the course nearer the centre of the wind bend, sails on a lift on both tacks; board D is headed on both tacks and loses out badly.

One-sided beats

Sometimes the beat is one-sided; in this case, always sail the long leg first. You will find it much easier to judge when to tack for the windward mark (point X in the figure above) when the mark is nearby. It is virtually impossible to judge your tack correctly if you're a leg away (point Y). Equally important, sailing the long tack first keeps you away from the lay line!

Sea breeze

Racing on a hot, sunny day, you should watch out for the effects of the sea breeze as the morning passes. The land is warmed by the sun; the air above it is heated and rises. Cold air is drawn in from the sea, creating a force 2 to 3 wind called a sea breeze.

If the prevailing (early morning) wind was on-

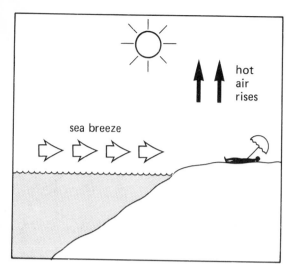

On a hot, sunny day an onshore sea breeze is created by the warm air rising over the land.

shore, the midday wind will be strong since the two winds add together. If the prevailing wind was off-shore, the two winds may cancel each other, result-ing in calm. If the wind was along the shore, the sea breeze will make it swing as shown in the figure below. Make sure you go up the left side of the beat to take advantage of this swing in the wind.

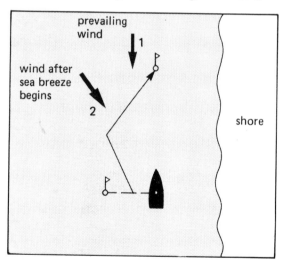

If the prevailing wind is along the shore, the sea breeze will cause it to swing to the direction of arrow 2.

Effects of the shore

For some reason comprehensible only to boffins the wind tends to cross the shoreline at right angles. This can be an advantage when beating near the shore. In the figure below, board A chooses the tack that takes it towards the shore; although initially sailing into a header, most of the journey will be in a lifting wind and board A will reach the windward mark well ahead of board B who sails the whole way in the prevailing wind.

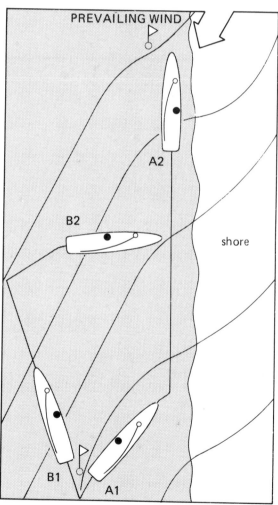

Beating near the shore: the inshore tack is better because the wind tends to cross the shore at right angles.

*Board 1974 is on port tack and must keep
clear of starboard tack boards.*

*Where two boards are on the same tack, the
windward board (2422) must keep clear.*

*Board 732 is tacking and has no rights over 26
until he has completed his tack.*

Avoiding protests on the beat

If your left hand is your mast hand you are on port
tack and must keep clear of starboard tack boards.
Methods of keeping clear are discussed on page 52.

If two boards are on the same tack (say both
have the right hand for their mast hand) the board to
windward must keep clear.

Be careful when tacking. While you're turning
you have no rights; even if you will be in the right
after your tack you have to tack in good time. Your
opponent doesn't have to begin to take avoiding
action until your tack is complete.

'Killing' the opposition on the beat

The sail of your board affects the wind in three
distinct ways, which in turn can affect boards sailing
near you. Use this knowledge to slow down your
rivals.

1 To leeward, there is an area shielded from the wind called the *windshadow*. This is devastating up to three mast lengths to leeward, but still has an effect about six mast lengths away.

2 The wind is 'broken up' as it passes over the sail, so behind the board there is an area of wind turbulence known as the 'hopeless position'!

3 Surprisingly, there is a problem area to windward as well. The wind is bent by the curve in the sail, and some is deflected to windward. This bounces onto the *wrong* side of the sail of a board to windward — he is being *lee-bowed*. This is a short-range effect, but within about one mast length it is deadly.

So, to 'attack' an opponent place yourself to windward, ahead, or ahead and to leeward. And naturally, try to avoid other boards doing the same to you!

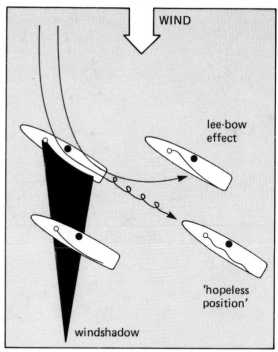

How your sail can disrupt the wind of boards sailing near you.

COVERING: ATTACK & DEFENCE

Covering is attacking one opponent by positioning your sail dead to windward of his sail, so that he falls into your windshadow. Some methods of getting an opponent's wind are shown on pages 50-51, together with the appropriate defence.

Once covering your opponent, you only have to tack every time he does to keep him in your windshadow. He will find it difficult to sail faster than you when you're cutting off his wind supply.

If these methods of defence fail and you find yourself being covered, try tacking often. To cover you, your opponent will have to tack just as often; you will both slow down and lose out relative to the rest of the fleet — after a while, he may realise this and let you go!

Covering on the beat: 692 has reached down to cover 1978 closely (but must keep clear).

Covering on the beat: the attacking board crosses ahead of 1974 and tacks to cover.

1974 tacks to get away, the tack beginning just as the other board completes his tack.

Loose covering

Usually, it is a mistake to single out one board and cover it. Your objective is to beat the whole fleet, not just one person. Tight cover is only worth while if you and one other board have a good lead, or if you only have to beat one rival to clinch a series.

Loose covering is a technique you can use to stay ahead of more than one board. Firstly, remember you must stay between your opponents and the next mark. Never sail out to one side of the group, but keep in the middle, tacking on windshifts. After a while, one board will emerge as more of a threat than the others. When a good shift comes, use it to sail over to his side of the course and apply tight cover until he drops back in line with the others.

Don't let your opponents disperse. If one looks like leaving the group and heading out to one side of the beat, sail over and apply tight cover, forcing him to tack back towards the others. Tack yourself, but don't cover him too closely — you want to encourage him back to the fold, not make him go off again!

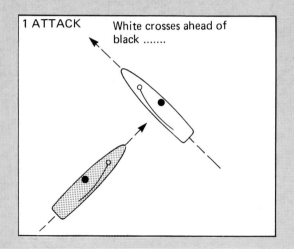

1 ATTACK White crosses ahead of black ....

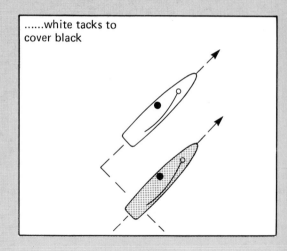

......white tacks to cover black

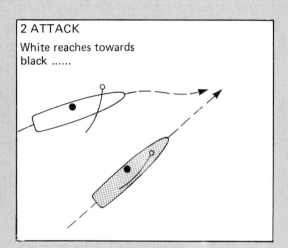

2 ATTACK

White reaches towards black ......

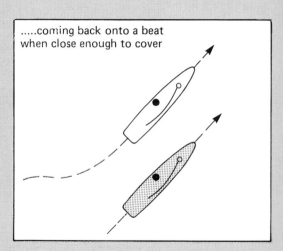

.....coming back onto a beat when close enough to cover

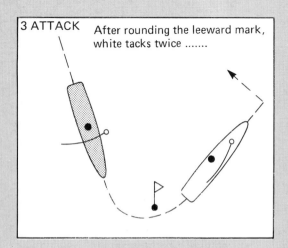

3 ATTACK After rounding the leeward mark, white tacks twice ....

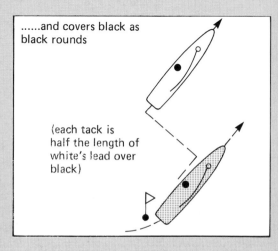

......and covers black as black rounds

(each tack is half the length of white's lead over black)

1 DEFENCE
Just as white completes his tack, black begins to tack the other way

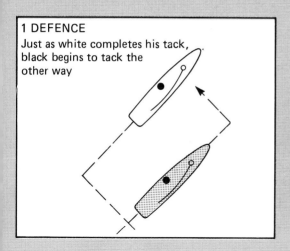

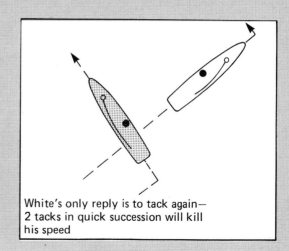

White's only reply is to tack again— 2 tacks in quick succession will kill his speed

2 DEFENCE
Black also gains speed by reaching

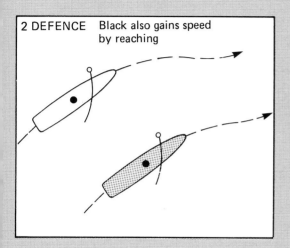

OR black can tack as white is reaching

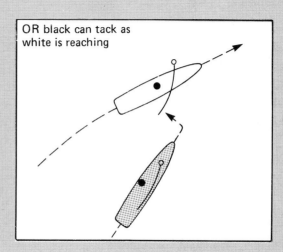

3 DEFENCE
Black rounds the mark........

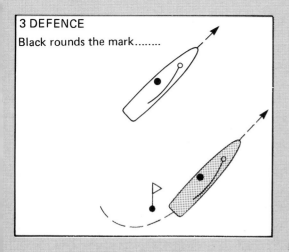

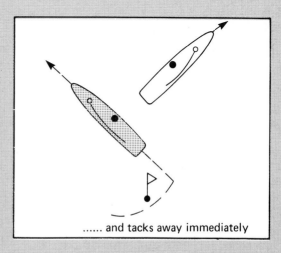

...... and tacks away immediately

Meeting on opposite tacks: it may be better for the starboard tack board to allow the port *tacker to cross in front; here 766 is allowed to cross although he has no rights.*

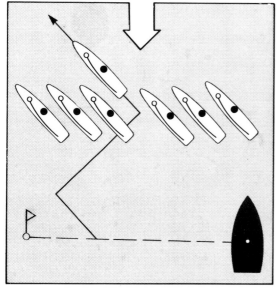

Always try to stay between the centre of the fleet and the next mark.

Sailing the fleet

Always try to stay between the centre of the fleet and the next mark. If you are in the lead after starting at the favoured end of a biased start line, it is essential to consolidate your position by tacking on the first good shift and sailing across to the centre of the fleet. Then tack again so that you're ahead and in control. This also has the advantage that you're not out on a limb on one side of the course, so whichever way the wind shifts you won't be wiped out by it.

Meeting on opposite tacks

Watch for other boards carefully through the window in your sail. If you are on port tack meeting a starboard tack board, you have the choice of keeping clear either by tacking or by bearing away behind the other board.

The advantages of tacking are small. If it is done very skilfully you may get a lee-bow on the starboard tack board; but both boards will lose ground

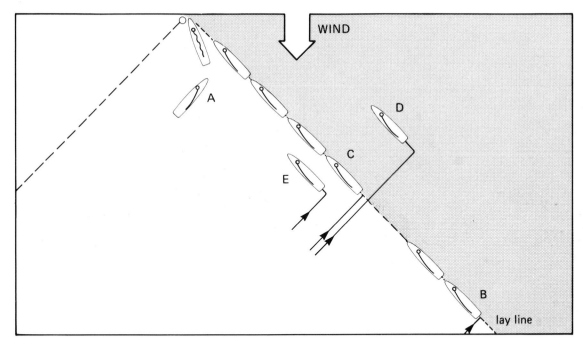

Rounding the windward mark (see text).

(you always do when you tack) and even if your tack is good, you will lose flexibility for some time, since you can't tack with the other board alongside. This manoeuvre really only pays off if you want to force the other board to the right (into adverse tide, for example) or shortly after the start, where if you duck behind one board you may then have to go behind several others. Remember that if you are sailing in waves, when you'll lose a lot of speed tacking, you'll need to be slightly ahead of the other board to risk tacking.

The advantages of bearing away are great. You won't lose much ground, provided you reach fast behind the other board and then luff a bit, and you are then free to sail your own race. Bearing away is, of course, essential if the right-hand side of the course is fastest.

If you are on starboard tack it will often pay to waive your rights and tell the port tacker to carry on across your bows. This prevents him tacking to leeward and is well worth it if the starboard tack is paying off (because of a windshift, for example).

THE WINDWARD MARK

Arriving at the windward mark is great if you're ahead. You can sail round it smugly watching the fleet follow.

If, as usual, you're a bit further back the mark can be an alarming experience. A great line of starboard tack boards builds up — if you leave it too late to join them and come in by the mark on port tack you often can't get in (like board A in the figure above). Joining the queue early (like board B) is safe but slow, because you are then in the hopeless position relative to the boards ahead.

The solution is to have a good look at that line of boards. If you reckon you can find a gap, come in on port and join the line late (board C). Otherwise it may be best to overstand the mark slightly and sail in outside the 'wall'. You then have speed enough and room to sail round the pile-up at the mark (board D).

Never tack to leeward of the 'wall' (like board E). In its windshadow you'll go so slowly that you'll

Starboard tackers approaching the windward mark.

never lay the mark — and you can't tack to clear it because of the other boards. Board E should have reached off through the gap, and then tacked behind D; E will lose a little ground by doing this — but will at least get round the mark!

THE REACH

Hammering down the reach gives you a real chance to put some daylight between yourself and the pack. Speed hints on the reach have been dealt with on pages 28-30; there are just two general points to make here.

Don't steer a straight course. In geometry, the shortest distance between two points is a straight line. True! But the *fastest* route on the reach is a 'wavy' course, luffing towards the wind in each lull and bearing away with each gust. In this way, you go up to meet each gust early, then ride with the gust as long as possible.

On a close reach, keep to windward. Sometimes the wind shifts so that one of the legs becomes a close reach; this means you have to pull the wishbone well in to sail to the next mark. In this case, sail well above the direct course — if the wind shifts further the reach becomes a beat and you need all the distance to windward you can get. Board X in the figure has followed this advice, but board Y has been caught by the windshift and can't lay the mark — in the end Y has to tack and loses a lot of time.

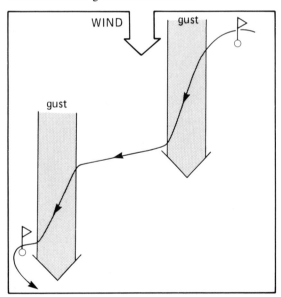

On the reach, it's fast to bear away in gusts, luffing up in the lulls, so as to ride the gusts as long as possible.

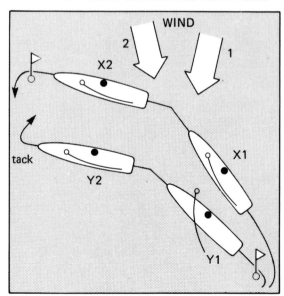

Keep to windward on a close reach in case the wind shifts further ahead.

1

2

Avoiding protests on the reach

Problems mainly occur on the reach when one board comes from behind and overtakes another to leeward or to windward.

Overtaking to leeward. You must keep clear of boards ahead of you. So in 1 in the photo sequence (left) the unnumbered board must keep clear. But once the boards are overlapped the rules change and the board to windward must keep clear. An overlap is established in 2 – the unnumbered board's bow passes ahead of an imaginary line extending from the aft edge of 1974. Thereafter 1974 must keep clear, although he must be given a fair chance to do so.

While the overlap exists, 1974 cannot bear off to prevent the other board from sailing through to leeward. When the boards are within three lengths of each other, 1974 must keep to his proper course (i.e. the fastest course to the next mark).

The unnumbered board cannot luff 1974 (turn into the wind and push 1974 off course) while the boards are overlapped. Once the overlap is broken (4) the unnumbered board can luff, and does so to ward off a counter-attack by 1974. The rules governing luffing are discussed below.

3

4

Overtaking another board to leeward.

5

6

7

Overtaking to windward. If an overtaking board tries to get past you to windward, you may try to prevent him by luffing as shown in the above photo sequence. This time 1974 overtakes the unnumbered board to windward. The latter luffs hard but 1974 gets by.

The unnumbered board can luff as quickly as he pleases, and even hit 1974 (who must try to keep clear — being to windward). The luffer can go head to wind, but may not tack. However, once 1974 shouts that he has gained a mast abeam position (centre) the leeward board must go back to his proper course and allow the other board to sail through to windward. The mast abeam position is defined as when the windward boardsailor, looking straight across his board, is in line with the leeward board's mast foot.

One other aspect of luffing is that you may not luff a windward board into an obstruction such as a rock or another right-of-way board. If you try, the windward board can shout 'water' and you must give it, going back to your proper course to the next mark.

And a further word of warning — if you're over-taking two boards, it is usually disastrous to sail

Overtaking another board to windward.

between them. Only do this if you're sure you can sail right through without getting hit.

What about the rest of the fleet?

So far we have assumed that you're so far ahead (or so far behind!) that you need not worry about the fleet. Usually, though, your tactics will depend on the boards around you. On a reach you have the problem of avoiding the windshadows of your competitors without being forced too far off course in doing so.

If you want to overtake a line of boards ahead you have two choices — sailing a windward or a leeward course; which you choose will depend on the type of reach.

Close reach

It is nearly impossible to overtake another board to leeward on a close reach because its windshadow

56

points backwards and you will sail straight into it and slow down. Your only hope is to go well to windward (to reduce the risk of being luffed).

Broad reach

It is usually better to sail a leeward course on a broad reach; you can almost pass a board in front before you are affected by its windshadow. This tactic is particularly effective when the boards ahead start luffing one another. They often go a long way off course, leaving you to sail a much shorter distance. You only need bear off far enough to avoid their windshadows (say six lengths to leeward). Choose your moment to bear off — preferably with a gust, and when there is a gap behind you (or the boards behind will take your wind).

A leeward course is even more effective if it gives you the inside turn at the next mark.

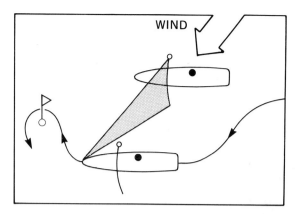

On a broad reach you can nearly pass the board in front before its windshadow will affect you. Here the leeward course will also give you the inside turn at the next mark.

Attacking one board

On a broad reach, work the puffs to close the gap. When you are about three lengths behind, wait until a gust comes and then luff. The gust will hit you first, pushing you to a position where you're blanketing your prey. (If someone tries this on you, anticipate his luff by luffing first.)

If the board ahead is wise to this trick, you can try overtaking to leeward. Once again, wait for a gust and bear off, using the other board's wake to surf on. Luff as you hit the tip of its windshadow and sail hard to try to get your nose ahead.

If you're really smart, you can 'feint' by luffing as though you're going to try to pass to windward. As the other board luffs in response, bear away; if the luff was too sharp it will slow him down and help you to get past.

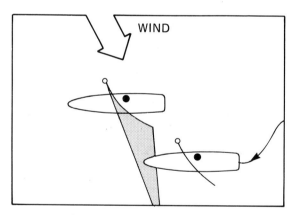

On a close reach the board's windshadow points backwards making overtaking to leeward virtually impossible.

True reach

If the wind is at right angles to the course, you can either go high or low. It's usually a mistake to sail straight — boards can overtake you to windward and leeward. Remember to keep between your rivals and the next mark, and to make sure you have that important inside turn at the mark.

A two-board race

If two of you are well ahead, you can indulge in this tactic. Go to windward of the other board; let him luff you — he'll think he's really clever as he takes you way out to the horizon. But what goes up must come down, and eventually he'll have to go for the mark. Now you're both on a run — with you right behind him cutting off his wind. Sail right up behind him and at the last minute turn off to the side that will give you an overlap at the mark.

Rounding the gybe mark: here the following board has an overlap just as the leader's bow is *two board lengths from the mark, giving the following board the right to the inside rounding.*

THE GYBE MARK

Go for the inside turn at the gybe mark (indeed, at any mark!). Boards outside you must give you room to gybe and sail round the mark, provided that you have achieved an overlap in time. The crucial moment is when the bow of the outside board is two lengths from the mark; if your bow is ahead of its stern at that moment, you're OK, but if you are further back than that you must keep clear as the other board rounds the mark.

THE RUN

Usually your main objective on the run is simply to survive! But if you can spare a few moments for tactics, you can gain a lot of places downwind.

Other things being equal, sail a straight course to the leeward mark. However, consider edging out to one side if you see a streak of wind there — this shows up as a dark patch spreading over the water. If you reckon a sea breeze is coming (see page 45)

make a large detour to be sure of catching it before the rest of the fleet.

As on a reach, it may pay you to luff slightly in lulls and bear away in gusts. This not only lets you ride the gust longer, but gives a flow of air over the sail in the lighter wind.

Avoiding protests on the run

1 Watch out for boards still on the beat. The only time *they* have to keep clear of *you* is if you are on starboard tack and they are on port tack. (Remember, you are on starboard tack when your right hand is your mast hand.)

2 If two boards are on the same tack (and not overlapped), the overtaking board must keep clear.

3 If two boards are on opposite tacks, the board on port tack must keep clear of the one on starboard.

4 While gybing, you must keep clear of other boards which are not.

5 Point 4 does not apply at the leeward mark — if you have an overlap you must be given room to round the mark, and this includes room to gybe.

Right of way on the run: 1974 is on port and must keep clear of the beating starboard tacker.

The overtaking board must keep clear.

Board 1974 is on port tack and must keep clear of the starboard tacker.

Keep clear of other boards when you are gybing.

'Killing' one board on the run

The run is the only part of the course where the cards are stacked against the leaders. You can come from behind to take their wind and there is very little they can do.

To attack one board in this way, you need to be within four mast lengths of your victim, with his board in line with your mast streamer — so that your sail will blanket his. Sail right up behind him, swerving aside to overtake at the last moment (think which side will give you the inside turn at the leeward mark). The other board's defence is to edge out to one side to avoid your blanketing zone. Simply follow him, keeping him in your sights.

If you find someone behind doing this to *you* — how unfair! — try alternately luffing and bearing away to keep clear air. If he follows you doggedly, the best tactic may be to let him overtake and then attack *him*. Usually you will lose less by this than by luffing to the horizon.

On the run your sail can cut off the wind of boards in front of you.

Sailing the fleet

In big fleets a 'wall' of boards can build up on the run. If the wind is light it is affected by this wall, tending to flow along it and round the edges. So stay on the edges of the wall to get the stronger wind there. If you are a short way ahead of a wall move out to one side to avoid being blanketed — choose the side which will give you the inside turn at the leeward mark.

If you have a good lead over a group of boards and want to play it safe, stay dead downwind of them; if they get a gust, you will (eventually) get it too.

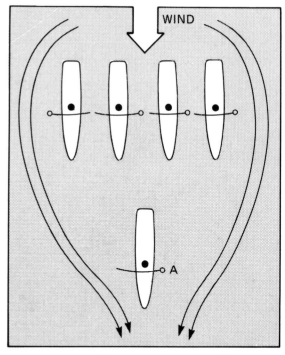

The wind tends to flow around the edges of a 'wall' of boards on the run. Board A should move to one side to get the stronger wind.

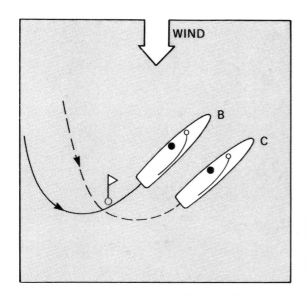

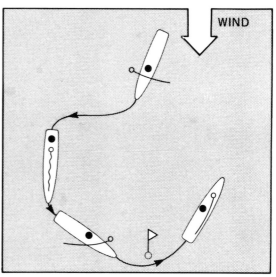

Board B rounds the leeward mark correctly; C loses ground by leaving it wide.

To avoid having to gybe as you round the leeward mark, luff up and gybe before you approach it.

THE LEEWARD MARK

Your objective is to round the leeward mark so that you *leave* it closely. To do this you must (a) sail the right course round the mark and (b) take the inside berth if there are several boards in contention.

The right course is to come in wide of the mark and almost clip the mark as you leave it. Coming in close and leaving it wide will lose you ground to windward.

If it is blowing hard and you're not sure you can gybe neatly at the mark, try luffing up and gybing well before the mark. You can then concentrate fully on the actual mark rounding and on steering through the crowd of boards that often collects at the leeward mark.

You must plan ahead to get the inside turn. If you round outside of a group of boards you will be in the hopeless position behind them at the beginning of the beat. It's better to slow down a little and cross behind the group — with a little bit of aggression you may be able to get the inside turn.

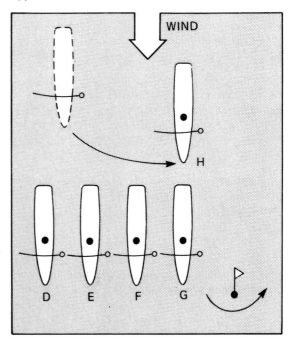

In a group of boards, it is better to slow down and go for a close rounding of the leeward mark (like board H) than to round on the outside (like D).

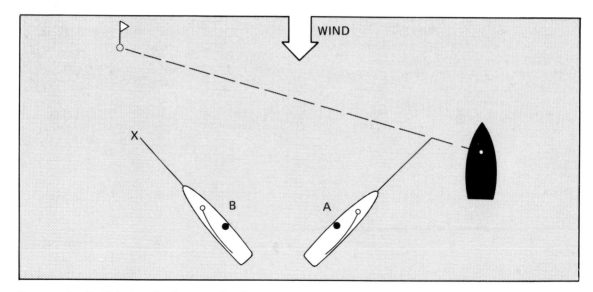

Crossing the finish line at the downwind end can make the difference between winning and losing.

THE FINISH

The finishing line is normally an imaginary line between the mast of the committee boat and a marker buoy. Unless the committee are very lucky, the finishing line will not be at right angles to the wind, and you should cross it near the *downwind* end — this shortens the distance you have to sail.

As you beat up to the finish try to judge which is the downwind end. If you can't, stay in the middle of the course and as soon as you can lay one end of the line, go for it. Board A in the figure above is following this advice; it can lay the committee boat so is finishing there; board B will have only reached point X as A finishes.

Finishing ahead of a bunch

If you find yourself ahead of a group of boards as you near the finishing line, it's important to stay between the centre of the bunch and the finish. Only let yourself get off-centre when you are near the line and when you are sure which end of the line you want to finish.

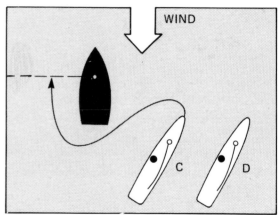

'Shutting the barn door'.

Finishing ahead of one other board

If you are ahead and there is only one other board to worry about, cover him to the finish.

If you are level with another board you may be able to manoeuvre him out of position by a tactic known as 'shutting the barn door'. Boards C and D in the figure above have been sailing neck and neck, but C has manoeuvred D 'outside' the finishing line. D can't tack without hitting C; the initiative lies with C, who can tack at will and cross the line first. Board C can even use this tactic if slightly behind D.

Avoiding protests at the finish

Although you finish when your bow hits the line, you are subject to the rules until you have cleared the line — either by sailing over it or by drifting back from it. So a collision on the finish line with a starboard tacker could disqualify you even after you had got the winning gun.

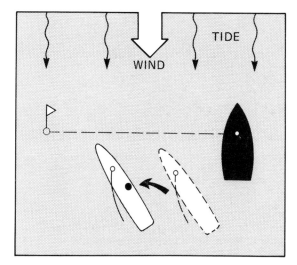

If the tide is against you, stay close to the line before the start, and allow for sideways drift.

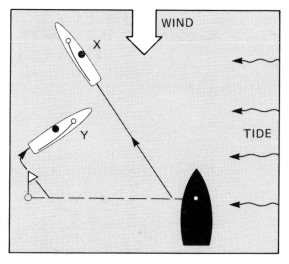

Start at the uptide end if the tide is along the line.

TIDES AND CURRENTS

Before you go afloat, find out what the tide will be doing while you are racing. The tide usually runs in each direction for six hours, flowing fastest at the midpoint (i.e. three hours before and three hours after high water).

On the course, check the tide as you go around each mark — you can see the wake downtide of the mark. If there is a strong tide running, tide tactics will be the most important part of your race plan.

At the start

Check the tide before the start by looking at the wake of the committee boat. If the tide is against you stay close to the line before the start: if the wind drops and you are far from the line you may never make the start. Line up early, sailing forwards at the same speed as the tide is pushing you back. You will find you can 'hang' on the line like this for several minutes — the only problem is that you drift slowly sideways, so begin well to the right of where you want to be when the gun goes.

If the tide is pushing you over the line, hang well back and go for the start at the last moment. Expect recalls!

If the tide is along the line, start at the uptide end. Board X in the figure will be well ahead of board Y who has to plug into the tide on port tack.

The beat

The tide runs most strongly in deep water, and is slowest in shallow water or near the shore; this is due to friction slowing the water as it 'rubs' against the land. So, when sailing against the tide, head inshore. Go right into bays — you may get a helpful back eddy there. Keep inshore until you are certain you can lay the mark — the last thing you want is to sail out into the strong tide too early and have to beat to the mark against it — if the breeze is light, you may never get round!

If the tide is with you on the beat then sail offshore into the strongest part of the tide — but be careful not to be swept past the windward mark!

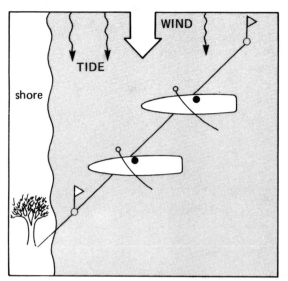

Using a transit to help sail directly to the mark.

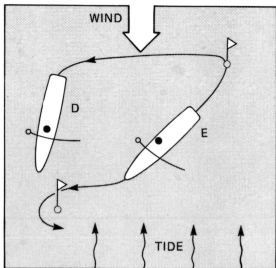

Board D has let himself be pushed well uptide of the mark and is forced to run slowly down to it against the tide.

The reach

As you start the reach, try to find a transit with the next mark; this will help you sail a straight course to the mark. You will need to head *uptide* of the direct course; the tide will carry you sideways as shown in the figure.

If the tide is pushing the fleet to windward you can gain a lot of places by taking a leeward course. What with the tide and the other boards luffing, many boards will find themselves way off course

(like board D) and having to run to the mark against the tide. Board E has played it more sensibly.

The run

The run is like the beat in reverse: with the tide behind you, sail offshore to get the most help from it. If the tide is against you, go inshore to cheat it. The lighter the wind, the more it is worth deviating from the straight course.

87654321